Introduction

William Wordsworth was bowled over by Barmouth when he visited the town in 1824. 'With a fine sea view in front, the mountains behind, the glorious estuary... Barmouth can always hold its own against any rival', he wrote. Many years later, television celebrity Julia Bradbury was equally impressed when, in 2008, she walked over Barmouth Bridge whilst filming her railway walk from Dolgellau. But it was from a viewpoint tucked away near Barmouth harbour that she indicated the tidal waters below. 'This is one of Wales' better kept secrets', she said.

Barmouth is, indeed, very special and its highly rated beach and dramatic surroundings attract visitors to the area in their thousands. But, for many, the town's less well known localities and buildings remain undiscovered. The first National Trust site, Dinas Oleu (Fortress of Light), four acres of steep hillside once described as 'Barmouth's open air sitting rooms', overlooks the town, yet gaining access to its paths and viewpoints is not straightforward. The attractive Old Town clings to the rock-face above the harbour in the manner of an Italian hill village, its houses connected by paths, not roads; yet many visitors remain unaware of its existence. Barmouth's medieval buildings, Llanaber Church and Ty Gwyn; the town's conservation park, Wern Mynach; The Birmingham Monument; the ruins of Gellfechan Farm; Orielton Woods: these wonderful places (and more) remain undiscovered by many visitors. Now, however, finding out about such places has been made easier through the creation of the twenty Barmouth walks contained in this book. The walks incorporate, and often link together, many of the town's less well-known localities and buildings, thus making them easier for visitors to discover, and delight in, for themselves.

Designed to be practical for those who want to spend an hour or two on a walk, rather than take an entire day, the walks are circular and are mostly quite short (up to 3½ miles, one 5 miles). The majority start in the centre of Barmouth at the railway station. Two other starting points, Orielton Woods (on the eastern edge of town) and the northern end of the promenade, are used for a few walks visiting locations nearby.

All of the walks can be undertaken by a reasonably fit person. Some are specially suitable for children. Stout shoes or walking boots, and waterproof clothing are recommended for all of them. A map of each walk is provided, together with detailed information on the precise route, linked to way-marks, gates, stiles, landmarks and other topographical features. The location of each route is shown on the back cover and a summary of the main characteristics and approximate length of each is shown on a chart. An estimated duration is also given but it is best to allow longer in order to linger over the many fine views and interesting places visited whilst on the walks.

Getting to Barmouth is straightforward. For car-drivers the town is on the A496 between Dolgellau and Harlech, and parking directions are provided in relation to each walk. Information about train and bus services is also included. In the case of those arriving by public transport, the railway station and is yards from the bus terminus. A weather forecast for this area is available at www.metoffice.gov.uk or www.bbc.co.uk/weather

Michael Burnett would like to thank the Pu____ ____il in Dolgellau for their help.

D1329344

CENTRAL BARMOUTH & DINAS OLEU

DESCRIPTION A fascinating 1½-mile walk which takes you to St John's Church and then to a famous National Trust site above Barmouth. It provides good views over the town's rooftops and harbour to Cardigan Bay. Allow one hour.

START Barmouth Railway Station (SH612158). Walk over the level-crossing and turn LEFT.

DIRECTIONS *From the east (A496): After entering the town, pass Barmouth Bridge (on the left) and then the Last Inn public house (on the right). Immediately after the pub turn LEFT under a railway bridge. Follow the road past the harbour and then, after a right turn, park in Barmouth's main car-park (on the RIGHT).*

From the north (A496): Drive through the town, continuing AHEAD at the end of the one-way system to pass St David's Church (on the right). Immediately after the church turn RIGHT under a railway bridge. Follow the road past the harbour and then, after a right turn, park in Barmouth's main car-park (on the RIGHT).

Bus services: Buses X94 (from Bala and Dolgellau) and 38 (from Harlech) serve Barmouth.

Train services: There are trains from Machynlleth, Porthmadog and Pwllheli.

I Walk away from the station, passing Talbot Place on your left. *There is an information board in Talbot Place, which is a pleasant landscaped square with seats in the centre of the town. Musical and other events are sometimes held here during the summer months.* At the junction with the High Street go RIGHT then LEFT over the pedestrian crossing. Then turn LEFT, cross Gellfechan Road and continue AHEAD on the right-hand pavement. Soon pass Lewis's Furniture Store (on the left).

2 When the road goes gently uphill and bends right, look out for a house named Isfryn on your right. *A short distance after Isfryn there are some stone and slate steps going up to the right.* Turn RIGHT and climb the steps (all 70 of them!) with St Tudwal's Catholic Church on your left. *This church was built in 1904-5 and you can see that it was constructed on a rock platform carved out of the cliff face, like St John's Church, which you'll pass later.*

3 When you reach the top of the steps go LEFT along the end of Bryn Awel Terrace then RIGHT up more steps to Gellfechan Road. *Bryn Awel Terrace was probably built to house workers in the local manganese mines. The remains of these mines can be found all over the hills above Barmouth. Gellfechan Road is named after a now ruined farm high in the hills above it.* Turn RIGHT here and follow the road along the back of Bryn Awel Terrace and uphill to the crest of the road. *There is a spectacular view from here over Barmouth and Cardigan Bay. You can see to the end of the Llŷn Peninsula and to Bardsey Island. The drop to the houses in King Edward's Street is almost vertical from here.*

4 Continue along the road as it goes downhill to the sharp right-hand bend just before St John's Church. *St John's is the biggest church in Barmouth. The foundation stone was laid in 1889 by Princess Beatrice, daughter of Queen Victoria, but, disastrously, the 100-ft tower collapsed two years later, in 1891. However, the tower was rebuilt and the church consecrated in 1895.*

5 Go AHEAD here, following Church Road alongside St John's and then past two houses up to the left. *There is a steep drop to the right of Church Road and a magnificent view over the rooftops of central Barmouth to the sea.* Continue AHEAD as the tarmac road becomes a tarmac path leading to an unsurfaced and narrow path. This soon descends, alongside railings, to another tarmac road.

6 Go LEFT here and follow the road uphill to its end alongside an information board. *You have now arrived at Dinas Oleu (The Fortress of Light). This was the first site to*

7 Looking seawards, go LEFT from the viewpoint then turn RIGHT to follow a walled track downhill. Walk down some steps then turn RIGHT along a path below a house. The path leads down to a road next to Drws y Mynydd house. Go down some steps and turn RIGHT onto the road. Follow the road downhill to a junction.

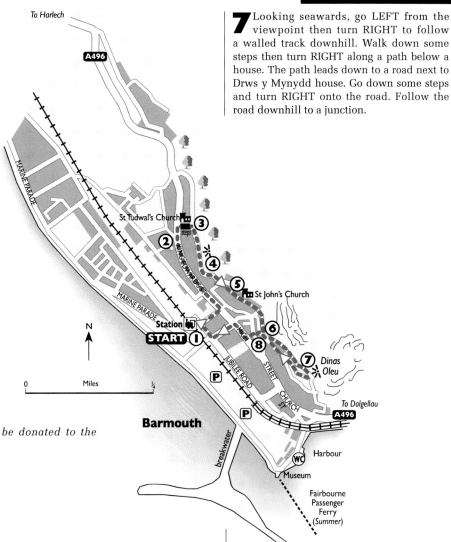

be donated to the

Barmouth

National Trust (by philanthropist Fanny Talbot in 1895). Dinas Oleu consists of over four acres of steep hillside with a network of paths. These paths link the hillside to mountain walks and to Barmouth town centre. There are extensive views from the information board over the town, the Mawddach Estuary, and Cardigan Bay.

8 Continue AHEAD here as the road goes steeply downhill. At a cross-roads go LEFT and walk down to a junction with Barmouth High Street. Cross the High Street at the nearby pedestrian crossing and turn RIGHT onto the pavement. Then go LEFT immediately after Christ Church Chapel. Continue AHEAD along this road and turn RIGHT just before the level-crossing to arrive back at the station.

WALK 2

ST JOHN'S CHURCH & THE ROCK

DESCRIPTION This 2-mile walk provides good views over Barmouth and Cardigan Bay and then, by contrast, takes you on a winding path through the attractive Old Town. Allow 1½ hours.

START Barmouth Railway Station (SH612158). Walk over the level-crossing and turn LEFT.

DIRECTIONS *From the east (A496):* After entering the town, pass Barmouth Bridge (on the left) and then the Last Inn public house (on the right). Immediately after the pub turn LEFT under a railway bridge. Follow the road past the harbour and then, after a right turn, park in Barmouth's main car-park (on the RIGHT).

From the north (A496): Drive through the town, continuing AHEAD at the end of the one-way system to pass St David's Church (on the right). Immediately after the church turn RIGHT under a railway bridge. Follow the road past the harbour and then, after a right turn, park in Barmouth's main car-park (on the RIGHT).

Bus services: Buses X94 (from Bala and Dolgellau) and 38 (from Harlech) serve Barmouth.

Train services: There are trains from Machynlleth, Porthmadog and Pwllheli.

1 Walk away from the station, passing Talbot Place on your left. At the first road junction cross the High Street, using the pedestrian crossing, and continue AHEAD into Gellfechan Road. Walk uphill as the road bends left then right to arrive at St John's Church. *St John's is the biggest church in Barmouth and was built during the 1890s.* Go RIGHT here, following Church Road to the right of St John's and then past two houses up to the left. *There is a steep drop to the right of Church Road and a magnificent view over the rooftops of central Barmouth to the sea.*

2 Continue AHEAD as the tarmac road becomes a tarmac path leading to an unsurfaced and narrow path. This soon descends, alongside railings, to another tarmac road. Go LEFT here and follow the road uphill to its end alongside an information board. *You have now arrived at Dinas Oleu (Fortress of Light), the first site to be donated to the National Trust (in 1895). There are extensive views from here over Barmouth, and over Cardigan Bay to Bardsey Island.*

3 Looking seawards, go LEFT from the viewpoint then turn RIGHT to follow a walled track downhill. Go down some steps, then LEFT and immediately RIGHT down more steps. *You are now in Barmouth Old Town (often called the Rock).* Turn sharp RIGHT at the next junction of paths, go down some steps then AHEAD at the next junction. Pass Carrera Cottage, then go down more steps.

4 Take the second LEFT (not the narrow path to nearby houses) at the following junction, then bear RIGHT, passing Gibraltar Cottage and going down more steps. Go sharp RIGHT at the next junction, where there's a small stone island containing plants. Go down more steps and bear LEFT to a narrow lane. Follow this the short distance to Barmouth High Street opposite St David's Church. *St David's was built in 1830 close to Barmouth's busy harbour.*

5 Turn RIGHT along the main road and follow it towards the centre of town, keeping on the right-hand side. Pass Barclay's Bank, on the left, then a chapel, now used as a restaurant and coffee shop, on the right, before taking the next road on the RIGHT (Cambrian Street). Go RIGHT at a crossroads and uphill, keeping LEFT at a junction. Pass the path (on the left) which you used earlier in the walk and then, soon after it, go LEFT onto another waymarked footpath.

6 Follow the path uphill as it becomes a track then passes through a wooden gate. At a junction of tracks go LEFT through a metal side gate adjoining a metal gate. Follow the track downhill past mine workings on

7 Turn RIGHT and follow the road downhill past a terrace of houses on the left. *This is Bryn Awel Terrace, which was probably built to house workers from the local manganese mines. The remains of these mines can be found all over the hills above Barmouth.* Continue downhill to the junction of Gellfechan Road with a main road.

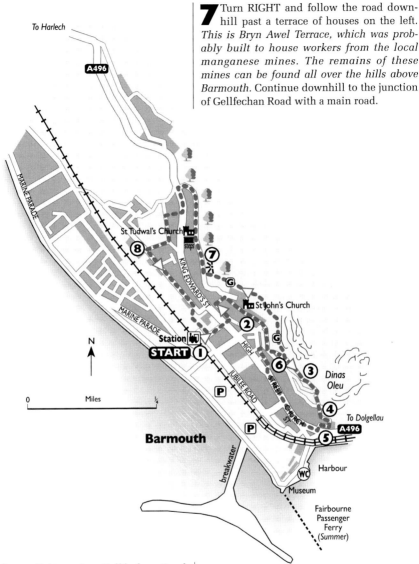

the right until it reaches Gellfechan Road alongside a waymark. *The waymark is for the Ardudwy Way, a long distance path which goes north from here to Harlech. You are now at the highest point on Gellfechan Road, which provides wonderful views. In good conditions, it's possible to make out Bardsey Island 20 miles away off the tip of the Llŷn Peninsula.*

8 Go LEFT here past the Bryn Teg pub. Cross the road when you see a path going off to the RIGHT. Follow this down some steps and AHEAD to a road. Turn LEFT and follow the road RIGHT to a junction. Go LEFT past Bradbury's Garage then HALF-RIGHT past the Co-op Supermarket to return to the starting point.

WALK 3

THE PROMENADE & HARBOUR

DESCRIPTION An interesting 1½-mile walk which takes you on the quickest route to the beach and out to the harbour entrance. You then explore the harbour itself before climbing to a wonderful viewpoint above the town. Allow one hour.

START (SH612158). Walk over the level-crossing and turn LEFT.

DIRECTIONS *From the east (A496):* After entering the town, pass Barmouth Bridge (on the left) and then the Last Inn public house (on the right). Immediately after the pub turn LEFT under a railway bridge. Follow the road past the harbour and then, after a right turn, park in Barmouth's main car-park (on the RIGHT).

From the north (A496): Drive through the town, continuing AHEAD at the end of the one-way system to pass St David's Church (on the right). Immediately after the church turn RIGHT under a railway bridge. Follow the road past the harbour and then, after a right turn, park in Barmouth's main car-park (on the RIGHT).

Bus services: Buses X94 (from Bala and Dolgellau) and 38 (from Harlech) serve Barmouth.

Train services: There are trains from Machynlleth, Porthmadog and Pwllheli.

1 With your back to the station turn RIGHT and then RIGHT again to go over the level-crossing. *The railway between Dolgellau, Barmouth and Pwllheli was opened in 1867. Today the crossing gates are operated by the train drivers themselves. Originally there was a signal box to the left on the far side of the crossing and it was the responsibility of the signalman to control the gates. At one time excursion trains brought thousands of visitors to Barmouth during the summer months.* Continue AHEAD until you reach the promenade.

2 Cross the road and turn LEFT here. Pass the Barmouth Lifeboat Station (on the left) and, soon after, take a sandy path going off to the RIGHT alongside a wall. Turn LEFT below a wooden statue on a sandy knoll. *The statue is reminiscent of the famous Easter Island figures and gazes steadfastly out to sea.* Continue along a concrete walkway to the northern entrance to the harbour. There is a flagpost here, marking the entrance. *The Mawddach Estuary is well known for its strong tidal flows and dangerous currents.*

3 Return, the way you came, to the promenade and turn RIGHT. Go LEFT across the road when you reach the Bath House restaurant (on the right). Continue AHEAD then bear RIGHT up some steps to arrive at Barmouth's old gaol, Ty Crwn (The Roundhouse). *This circular stone building was used to house troublemakers during the first half of the 19thC. The building went out of use in 1861, when a police station opened in Barmouth. It was rebuilt during the 1980s as a legacy of the past.*

4 Follow the road going downhill from Ty Crwn to the harbour, passing the Davy Jones' Locker restaurant. *Once an important harbour, Barmouth is now largely the preserve of small sailing boats. A well-known yacht race, The Three Peaks Race, starts from here each summer.* Turn LEFT and follow the road alongside the harbour, going under a railway bridge. Turn LEFT at the next junction and pass St David's Church. *St David's was built in 1830 close to Barmouth's busy port.* Cross the road, turn LEFT and continue AHEAD on the right-hand pavement when the road divides.

5 Pass Barclay's Bank, on the left, then a chapel, now used as a restaurant and coffee shop, on the right. Continue past Walter Lloyd Jones, the estate agents and auctioneers, on the right. Immediately after a Spar shop, on the left, turn RIGHT and follow Gellfechan Road as it twists and turns uphill past St John's Church (on the right). *St John's is the biggest church in Barmouth and was built during the 1890s.*

7 Follow the road downhill then past a row of houses on the left. *This is Bryn Awel Terrace, which was probably built to house workers from the local manganese mines. The remains of these mines can be found all over the hills above Barmouth.* Turn LEFT at the end of the terrace and go down some steep steps to the main Barmouth to Harlech main road (take care here as the pavement is narrow and the road busy).

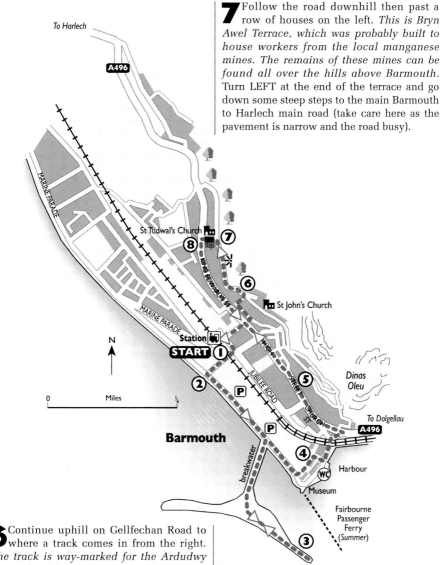

6 Continue uphill on Gellfechan Road to where a track comes in from the right. *The track is way-marked for the Ardudwy Way, a long distance path which goes north to Harlech. You are now at the highest point on Gellfechan Road, from where there is a wonderful view. The drop to the houses in King Edward's Street is almost vertical from here, and it's possible to make out Bardsey Island, off the tip of the Llŷn Peninsula, in good conditions.*

8 Turn LEFT and follow the road downhill towards the town centre. Pass Lewis' Furniture Store (on the right) and the junction with Park Road (also on the right). Cross Gellfechan Road and go RIGHT over the pedestrian crossing. Then turn RIGHT and LEFT to pass Talbot Place and return to the start.

DINAS OLEU & THE FRENCHMAN'S GRAVE

DESCRIPTION There are spectacular views on this 2-mile walk during which you to visit a National Trust viewpoint high above Barmouth's old town. Allow 1½ hours.
START (SH612158). Walk over the level-crossing and turn LEFT.
DIRECTIONS *From the east (A496):* After entering the town, pass Barmouth Bridge (on the left) and then the Last Inn public house (on the right). Immediately after the pub turn LEFT under a railway bridge. Follow the road past the harbour and then, after a right turn, park in Barmouth's main car-park (on the RIGHT).
From the north (A496): Drive through the town, continuing AHEAD at the end of the one-way system to pass St David's Church (on the right). Immediately after the church turn RIGHT under a railway bridge. Follow the road past the harbour and then, after a right turn, park in Barmouth's main car-park (on the RIGHT).
Bus services: Buses X94 (from Bala and Dolgellau) and 38 (from Harlech) serve Barmouth.
Train services: There are trains from Machynlleth, Porthmadog and Pwllheli.

I Walk away from the station, passing Talbot Place on your left. At the first road junction cross the High Street, using the pedestrian crossing, and continue AHEAD into Gellfechan Road. Walk uphill as the road bends left then right to arrive at St John's Church. *St John's is the biggest church in Barmouth and was built during the 1890s.* Continue uphill on Gellfechan Road to where a waymarked track comes in from the right. *You are now at the highest point on Gellfechan Road from where there is a wonderful view. The drop to the houses in King Edward's Street is almost vertical from here.* Turn RIGHT and follow the track uphill. Look to the left as you walk to see the first

of two tunnel entrances. *This area was once extensively mined for manganese.*

2 Go through the side gate adjoining a metal gate and turn LEFT. Soon you'll pass the second tunnel entrance (on the right) before bearing right as the track climbs more steeply. When the track divides continue AHEAD. *The left turn here is way-marked for the Ardudwy Way, a long distance path which goes north to Harlech. Leaflets about the path are available in the Barmouth Tourist Information Centre.* Soon the track levels off and goes through a wooden gate. The track then bends right and you'll see a gate through the wall on the right. Go RIGHT through the gate to the National Trust viewpoint below. *You are now high on the hillside of Dinas Oleu (Fortress of Light). This was the first site to be donated to the National Trust (by philanthropist Fannie Talbot, in 1895). A plaque on the wall of the viewpoint commemorates the 100th anniversary of the donation. There are extensive views from here over Barmouth, the Mawddach Estuary, and over Cardigan Bay to Bardsey Island.*

3 Continue past the viewpoint and bear LEFT behind it, then turn LEFT to join a path which goes downhill. At a junction of paths go LEFT and continue downhill. After going down some steps you'll meet a path at right-angles. Go LEFT onto this path and walk uphill through a metal gate. After a short distance you'll see a gate on the right marked 'Frenchman's Grave'. Go through and downhill before the path levels off and arrives at a second gate. The grave is just after this. *The Frenchman, Auguste Guyard, settled in Barmouth Old Town and loved the area so much that he wished to be buried here. A poem on a plaque marks his grave. There is a good view over Barmouth Harbour from here.*

4 Return to the upper gate, go through and turn LEFT to retrace your steps. Once through the wooden gate continue AHEAD, ignoring a path going off right. Walk downhill on a grassy path, bear LEFT at a junction and then RIGHT at a second junction. Go

5 Looking seawards, go LEFT from the viewpoint then turn RIGHT to follow a walled track downhill. Walk down some steps then turn RIGHT along a path below a house. The path leads down to a narrow road next to Drws y Mynydd house. Go down some steps and turn RIGHT onto the road. Follow the road down to a junction.

6 Turn sharp RIGHT here then immediately go LEFT onto a path alongside some railings. Follow the path to join the tarmac road which runs alongside St John's Church. *St David's was built in 1830 and is the oldest*

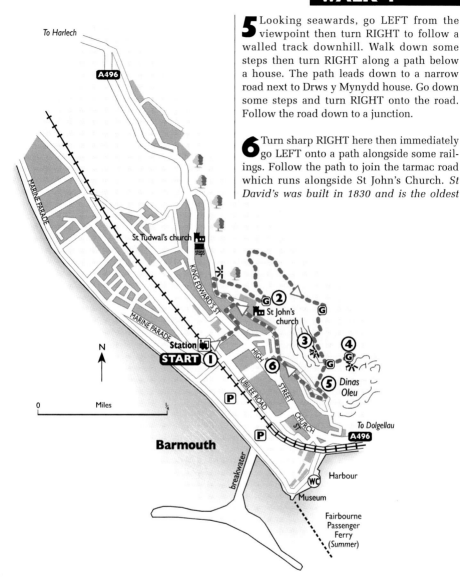

down two steps and past a National Trust sign to a road. Turn LEFT to arrive at an information board. *Fannie Talbot lived in the original Ty'n Ffynnon house nearby (the original was destroyed in a fire).*

church in Barmouth. At the road junction just beyond the church go LEFT and follow Gellfechan Road as it winds downhill to its junction with Barmouth High Street. Cross the High Street, using the pedestrian crossing. Then turn RIGHT and LEFT to pass Talbot Place and return to thestart.

WERN MYNACH & GELLFECHAN ROAD

DESCRIPTION This fascinating 1½-mile walk take you to places associated with the Monks of Cymer Abbey and to one of Barmouth's hidden secrets, a conservation park where specially planted trees and shrubs grow in glorious profusion. The walk concludes with a visit to a spectacular view-point just above the centre of the town. Allow one hour.

START Barmouth Railway Station (SH612158). Walk over the level-crossing and turn LEFT.

DIRECTIONS *From the east (A496):* After entering the town, pass Barmouth Bridge (on the left) and then the Last Inn public house (on the right). Immediately after the pub turn LEFT under a railway bridge. Follow the road past the harbour and then, after a right turn, park in Barmouth's main car-park (on the RIGHT.

From the north (A496): Drive through the town, continuing AHEAD at the end of the one-way system to pass St David's Church (on the right). Immediately after the church turn RIGHT under a railway bridge. Follow the road past the harbour and then, after a right turn, park in Barmouth's main car-park (on the RIGHT).

Bus services: Buses X94 (from Bala and Dolgellau) and 38 (from Harlech) serve Barmouth.

Train services: There are trains from Machynlleth, Porthmadog and Pwllheli.

❚ With your back to the station turn RIGHT, and then RIGHT again, to go over the level crossing. *The railway between Dolgellau, Barmouth and Pwllheli was opened in 1867.* Continue AHEAD until you reach the promenade. Cross the road, turn RIGHT and follow the promenade for a short distance, passing the Arbour Hotel (on the right). Cross the road by the Barmouth Coastguard Rescue Station (on the right) and follow the minor road leading away from the sea-front just by it.

2 At a T-junction bear HALF-RIGHT across the road beyond and walk over the level-crossing AHEAD. Follow the road leading away from the crossing but soon go LEFT through a stone gateway and LEFT again to follow a road alongside Barmouth football ground. At the end of the football pitch bear RIGHT and walk between two enormous, vertical slate slabs to enter Barmouth's Wern Mynach Park. *Wern Mynach means 'The marshland belonging to the monks', and this is one of many sites in the Barmouth area named after the Cistercian monks of Cymer Abbey. The ruins of the abbey can be seen at Llanelltyd, near Dolgellau. The monks brought their animals to the area during the winter to graze on the salt marshes. You will follow Ffordd Mynach (Road of the Monks) later in this walk. The urban green space you have entered has been created by the Barmouth Environmental Conservation Group and contains specially planted species of trees and shrubs.*

3 Bear LEFT and pass a large wooden model of a sailing boat on your left. *The boat is named 'Mynach' and is accessible to visiting children.* Turn RIGHT just past a wooden gate *(the path beyond the gate itself takes you through a wonderful tunnel of trees to a cleared space with seats suitable for a picnic).* Then follow an unmade path past a pond on the left. Bear LEFT at a junction of paths and then go LEFT again onto a tarmac path. Pass another pond, then immediately turn RIGHT and walk uphill. When confronted by a wall go RIGHT up some steps alongside a metal hand-rail then past a gate marked 'private'. Continue uphill and go LEFT to a main road.

4 Turn LEFT onto the footpath on the left of the road and follow it past Brook House (on the left). Then cross the main road and bear RIGHT to join Ffordd Mynach *(another reference to the Monks of Cymer Abbey)* at its junction with the main road. Follow Ffordd Mynach, ignoring another road going left. Pass Barmouth Rectory (on the left), and then two tracks

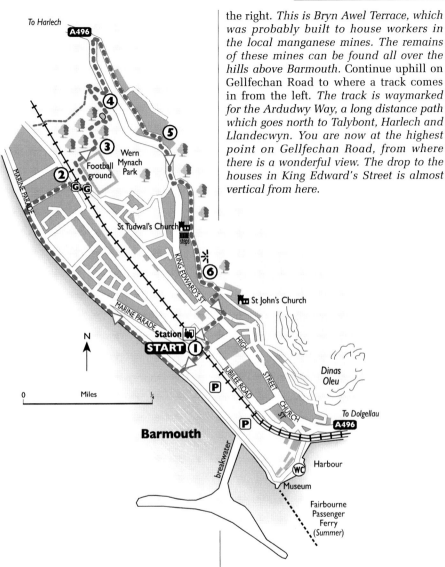

To Harlech

A496

Marine Parade

To Harlech

4

5

3

Wern
Mynach
Park

Football
ground

2

G G

St Tudwal's Church
steps

King Edward's St

6

St John's Church

Marine Parade

N

Station

START

Miles

0   ¼

Jubilee Road

High Street

Church St

P

P

Dinas
Oleu

To Dolgellau

A496

Barmouth

breakwater

WC   Harbour

Museum

Fairbourne
Passenger
Ferry
(Summer)

the right. *This is Bryn Awel Terrace, which was probably built to house workers in the local manganese mines. The remains of these mines can be found all over the hills above Barmouth.* Continue uphill on Gellfechan Road to where a track comes in from the left. *The track is waymarked for the Ardudwy Way, a long distance path which goes north to Talybont, Harlech and Llandecwyn. You are now at the highest point on Gellfechan Road, from where there is a wonderful view. The drop to the houses in King Edward's Street is almost vertical from here.*

going to the left as Ffordd Mynach goes downhill to the Glencairn bed and breakfast establishment (on the left).

5 Soon after this Ffordd Mynach joins the main road. Go LEFT and follow the main road the short distance to the Bryn Teg pub. Take Gellfechan Road, on the LEFT just before the pub, and follow it uphill. Soon pass a row of houses on

6 Follow the road steeply downhill to St John's Church. *St John's is the biggest church in Barmouth and was built during the 1890s.* Then turn RIGHT and follow Gellfechan Road as it winds downhill to its junction with Barmouth High Street. Go over the pedestrian crossing, then RIGHT and LEFT, to return to the start.

WALK 6

LLANABER CHURCH

DESCRIPTION This fascinating 3-mile walk takes you north along the coast to the ancient parish church of Barmouth at Llanaber. The church is in a glorious setting where there magnificent views along the coast and out to the end of the Llŷn Peninsula. Allow 3 hours.

START Barmouth Railway Station (SH612158). Walk over the level-crossing and turn LEFT.

DIRECTIONS *From the east (A496):* After entering the town, pass Barmouth Bridge (on the left) and then the Last Inn public house (on the right). Immediately after the pub turn LEFT under a railway bridge. Follow the road past the harbour and then, after a right turn, park in Barmouth's main car-park (on the RIGHT).

From the north (A496): Drive through the town, continuing AHEAD at the end of the one-way system to pass St David's Church (on the right). Immediately after the church turn RIGHT under a railway bridge. Follow the road past the harbour and then, after a right turn, park in Barmouth's main car-park (on the RIGHT).

Bus services: Buses X94 (from Bala and Dolgellau) and 38 (from Harlech) serve Barmouth.

Train services: There are trains from Machynlleth, Porthmadog and Pwllheli.

I With your back to the station turn RIGHT and then RIGHT again to go over the level crossing. *The railway between Dolgellau, Barmouth and Pwllheli was opened in 1867.* Continue AHEAD until you reach the promenade. Cross the road and turn RIGHT here. *Much of the sea-wall which protects Barmouth and its promenade was built during the 1930s.* Follow the footpath along the left of the promenade, passing the Arbour Hotel (on the right). Then pass the Barmouth School playing field with its wind turbine (on the right). *This wind turbine provides electricity for the school.* The Min y Mor Hotel, with its impressive tower, comes soon after the playing field (also on the right). *The white building on the corner of the next road on the right is the Barmouth Coastguard Rescue Station.*

2 Continue along the footpath (or, if the tide is out, along the beach) until you reach the end of the promenade. *There are magnificent views of the Llŷn Peninsula as you walk. Bardsey Island, off the western tip of the Peninsula, can also be made out in clear conditions.* Follow the sea-wall to the RIGHT here, passing a mini-roundabout (on the right). Then turn LEFT before the level-crossing and walk over the wall using the steps provided. Bear RIGHT then LEFT to walk along the high bank of stones and shingle next to the railway line (to the right). Soon join a concrete path alongside the sea-wall (on the left) and follow the path to a footbridge over the railway. Go up and down steps, then walk over the bridge. Follow the path beyond it up to a main road.

3 Turn LEFT and follow the footpath alongside the road. Pass an entrance to Llanaber cemetery (on the left) then walk LEFT through the gateway into the church-yard. Follow the path AHEAD to the church itself. *St Bodfan's and St Mary's Church is the finest 13thC church in Gwynedd. Its location, with views from the churchyard out over Cardigan Bay and along the coast to north and south, is spectacular. The church houses two ancient Christian inscribed stones discovered in the locality.*

4 Return the way you came to the road. *(It is possible to return to Barmouth by train from the nearby Llanaber Station. To get there take a path on the LEFT as you walk away from the church. Then go LEFT through a gate onto the footpath alongside the road. Follow the path for a short distance then go LEFT downhill on a track and through a gate to the station. Do check train times beforehand though; and remember you need to give a signal to the driver from the platform.)* Turn RIGHT and walk along the right-hand pavement past the path from the railway bridge. Continue alongside the road past a church hall. Ignore a road, way-marked for the Wales Coast Path, going right. Ignore a footpath sign (on the left) and pass a lay-by (on the right) before going RIGHT downhill on a way-marked path. Turn RIGHT onto a road alongside Minafon House (on the

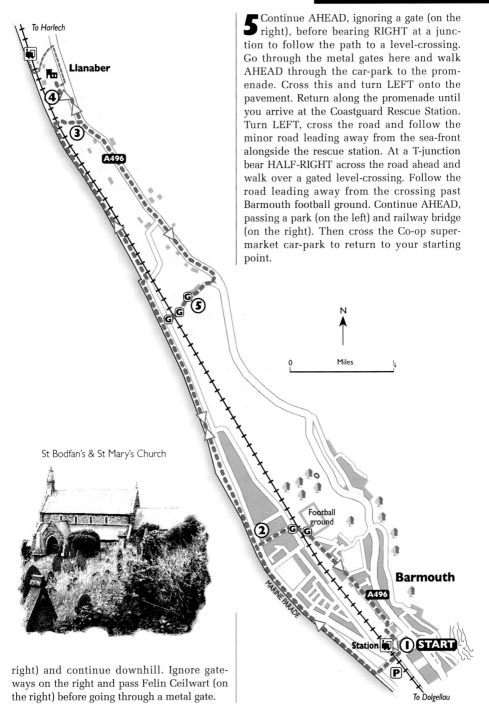

5 Continue AHEAD, ignoring a gate (on the right), before bearing RIGHT at a junction to follow the path to a level-crossing. Go through the metal gates here and walk AHEAD through the car-park to the promenade. Cross this and turn LEFT onto the pavement. Return along the promenade until you arrive at the Coastguard Rescue Station. Turn LEFT, cross the road and follow the minor road leading away from the sea-front alongside the rescue station. At a T-junction bear HALF-RIGHT across the road ahead and walk over a gated level-crossing. Follow the road leading away from the crossing past Barmouth football ground. Continue AHEAD, passing a park (on the left) and railway bridge (on the right). Then cross the Co-op supermarket car-park to return to your starting point.

To Harlech

Llanaber

A496

St Bodfan's & St Mary's Church

N

0   Miles   ¼

Football ground

Barmouth

A496

MARINE PARADE

Station   **START**

To Dolgellau

right) and continue downhill. Ignore gateways on the right and pass Felin Ceilwart (on the right) before going through a metal gate.

WALK 7

DINAS OLEU & THE ARDUDWY WAY

DESCRIPTION On this fascinating 2-mile walk you visit a National Trust site and then continue on a wonderful footpath across the hillside directly above Barmouth. Allow 2 hours.

START Barmouth Railway Station (SH612158). Walk over the level-crossing and turn LEFT.

DIRECTIONS *From the east (A496):* After entering the town, pass Barmouth Bridge (on the left) and then the Last Inn public house (on the right). Immediately after the pub turn LEFT under a railway bridge. Follow the road past the harbour and then, after a right turn, park in Barmouth's main car-park (on the RIGHT.

From the north (A496): Drive through the town, continuing AHEAD at the end of the one-way system to pass St David's Church (on the right). Immediately after the church turn RIGHT under a railway bridge. Follow the road past the harbour and then, after a right turn, park in Barmouth's main car-park (on the RIGHT).

Bus services: Buses X94 (from Bala and Dolgellau) and 38 (from Harlech) serve Barmouth.

Train services: There are trains from Machynlleth, Porthmadog and Pwllheli.

I Walk away from the station, passing Talbot Place on your left. At the first junction turn RIGHT then cross the High Street at the pedestrian crossing and turn RIGHT. Take the first LEFT (Water Street) and follow the road to a cross-roads. Turn LEFT and walk uphill to a junction. Bear RIGHT here and continue uphill. Soon you'll see a path, marked Dinas Oleu (Fortress of Light), going LEFT from the road alongside Drws y Mynydd house. Follow this path uphill, past a house (on the left). Then turn LEFT up some steps next to another Dinas Oleu marker. Follow this path uphill between walls and then go LEFT to an information board about Dinas Oleu. *Philanthropist Fannie*

Talbot donated the hillside of Dinas Oleu to the National Trust in 1895. There are extensive views from here over Barmouth, the Mawddach Estuary, and over Cardigan Bay to Bardsey Island.

2 With your back to the sea, walk uphill away from the information board past a National Trust sign. Bear LEFT at a junction of paths above some steps. At the next junction bear LEFT and walk uphill past a stone seating area (on the right). Continue uphill, sometimes using steps, and then go LEFT at the next junction. The path then descends past a stone seat (on the right) and down steps to another junction. Turn LEFT here and follow a zig-zag path downhill, often using steps. At a junction with a track next to a high fence turn RIGHT and follow the track uphill. Go through a wooden gate and bear RIGHT at a junction of tracks where there's a metal gate on the left. Soon you'll pass a tunnel entrance (on the right). *This area was once extensively mined for manganese.* Then the track bears RIGHT at a spectacular viewpoint. *Pause here to take in the views along the coast, and out to the end of the Llŷn Peninsula. The track you are now on is part of the Ardudwy Way, a long distance path which goes north from here to Talybont and Harlech.*

3 Retrace your steps to the metal gate and go RIGHT through the side gate adjoining it. Go downhill, passing a section of wall (on the right). *Look for a second mine entrance just beyond the wall.* Continue AHEAD, ignoring a path going left, to a junction with a road, and turn RIGHT. *You are now at the highest point on Gellfechan Road. The drop to the houses in King Edward's Street is almost vertical from here.* Walk downhill on Gellfechan Road, soon passing a terrace of houses on the left. *This is Bryn Awel Terrace, which was probably built to house workers from the local manganese mines.* Continue along the road which descends steeply to a junction with a main road alongside the Bryn Teg pub.

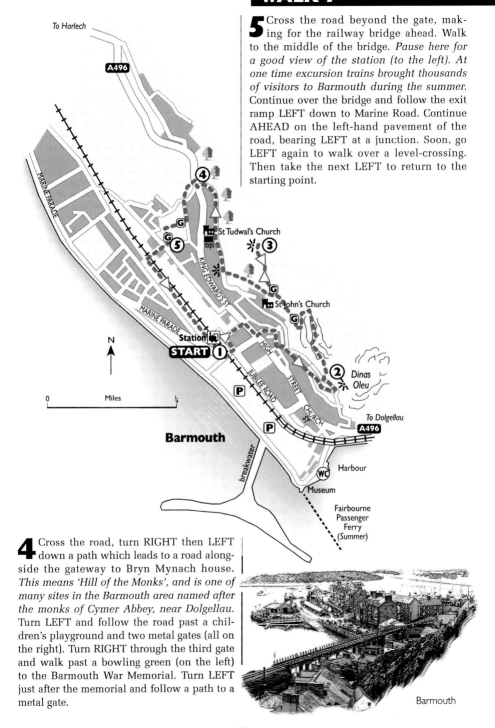

5 Cross the road beyond the gate, making for the railway bridge ahead. Walk to the middle of the bridge. *Pause here for a good view of the station (to the left). At one time excursion trains brought thousands of visitors to Barmouth during the summer.* Continue over the bridge and follow the exit ramp LEFT down to Marine Road. Continue AHEAD on the left-hand pavement of the road, bearing LEFT at a junction. Soon, go LEFT again to walk over a level-crossing. Then take the next LEFT to return to the starting point.

To Harlech

A496

MARINE PARADE

④

G

G ⑤

St Tudwal's Church

steps

⚒ ③

King Edward's St

G

Marine Parade

St John's Church

G

Station

START ①

High Street

N

② Dinas Oleu

Jubilee Road

P

Church St

0 Miles ¼

Barmouth

breakwater

To Dolgellau

A496

P

WC Harbour

Museum

Fairbourne Passenger Ferry (Summer)

4 Cross the road, turn RIGHT then LEFT down a path which leads to a road alongside the gateway to Bryn Mynach house. *This means 'Hill of the Monks', and is one of many sites in the Barmouth area named after the monks of Cymer Abbey, near Dolgellau.* Turn LEFT and follow the road past a children's playground and two metal gates (all on the right). Turn RIGHT through the third gate and walk past a bowling green (on the left) to the Barmouth War Memorial. Turn LEFT just after the memorial and follow a path to a metal gate.

Barmouth

SCULPTURES & A ROUND HOUSE

DESCRIPTION A level one-mile walk which takes you the harbour and visits several of Barmouth's famous land-marks. The walk is particularly suitable for children. Allow one hour.

START Barmouth Railway Station (SH612158). Walk over the level-crossing and turn LEFT.

DIRECTIONS *From the east (A496): After entering the town, pass Barmouth Bridge (on the left) and then the Last Inn public house (on the right). Immediately after the pub turn LEFT under a railway bridge. Follow the road past the harbour and then, after a right turn, park in Barmouth's main car-park (on the RIGHT).*

From the north (A496): Drive through the town, continuing AHEAD at the end of the one-way system to pass St David's Church (on the right). Immediately after the church turn RIGHT under a railway bridge. Follow the road past the harbour and then, after a right turn, park in Barmouth's main car-park (on the RIGHT).

Bus services: Buses X94 (from Bala and Dolgellau) and 38 (from Harlech) serve Barmouth.

Train services: There are trains from Machynlleth, Porthmadog and Pwllheli.

1 With your back to the station, turn RIGHT. Cross the road ahead and walk along the right-hand pavement of Jubilee Road. Pass the Theatr y Ddwraig/Dragon Theatre (on the left). *This popular community theatre is a converted Victorian chapel.* Soon arrive at the first of several sculptures (on the right) visited on this walk. *This is a wooden sculpture of a mother and baby seal, lying on a stone and shingle bank.*

2 Continue AHEAD alongside the railway. Go LEFT then RIGHT to Cumberland Place. Turn LEFT here by a marker and then RIGHT alongside St David's Church. Pass the Inglenook Restaurant (on the right) and bear LEFT across the road ahead to a marble sculpture. *The sculpture is called 'The Last Haul'. Other objects of interest here are a*

canon and a ship's anchor. Walk below the railway bridge near the sculpture towards Barmouth Harbour.

3 Pass the Sailor's Institute and bear LEFT to the harbour-side. *There's a ferry*

WALK 9

Barmout

across the harbour from here, and wonderful views of Barmouth Bridge and Cadair Idris. Retrace your steps, cross the road and walk uphill alongside Davy Jones' Locker Restaurant. *On your right is Ty Gwyn, a medieval building housing a maritime exhibition.* Continue AHEAD to Ty Crwn (The Roundhouse). *This stone building was used to house troublemakers during the 19thC.*

4 Walk down steps from Ty Crwn towards the sea. Cross the road ahead to join the promenade. Go RIGHT, then LEFT along a sandy path near a wall. Soon reach a wooden sculpture on a sandy knoll. *This statue is reminiscent of the famous Easter Island figures.* Go LEFT to the harbour entrance. Return to the promenade and go LEFT. Turn RIGHT across the road and then LEFT near the the Lifeboat Station. *There is a shop and information centre here.* Go AHEAD then RIGHT to return to your starting point.

WALK 9

FROM MONKS TO COASTGUARDS

DESCRIPTION This easy one-mile walk visits a Barmouth conservation park and the town's Coastguard Rescue Station on the sea-front. The walk is particularly suitable for children. Allow one hour.

START, DIRECTIONS, Bus & Train sevices: See Walk 8 opposite.

St Tudwal's Church

N

0   Miles   ¼

St John's Church

WARD'S ST

ation

① START

HIGH STREET

Dinas Oleu

P

②

CHURCH ST

P

To Dolgellau
A496

breakwater

④

③

WC

Harbour

WALK 8

Museum

Fairbourne
Passenger
Ferry
(Summer)

With your back to the Tourist Information Centre turn RIGHT and then RIGHT again over the level-crossing. Go RIGHT, then RIGHT into Marine Road. Walk on the right-hand pavement and then RIGHT onto a railway bridge. *Pause here for a good view of* the station *(to the right). At one time summer excursion trains brought thousands of visitors to Barmouth.*

2 Walk over the bridge, cross the road beyond and walk through a metal gate HALF-LEFT to Barmouth War Memorial. Go RIGHT past a bowling green (on the right), through another metal gate and turn LEFT. Pass two gates and a children's playground (all on the left). Go RIGHT alongside the entrance to Bryn Mynach (Hill of the Monks) house. Walk uphill to a road, turn LEFT and pass a metal gate (on the left). *The house with a tower on the left is a prominent Barmouth landmark, Tŵr Mynach (Tower of the Monks).* Continue alongside a metal fence to a waymark.

3 Go LEFT, past a gate (on the right) and down steps. Turn LEFT to a junction near a pond. You are now in Wern Mynach (The Monks' Marshland) conservation park. *This is another of the sites in Barmouth named after the monks of Cymer Abbey near Dolgellau.* Turn RIGHT alongside a stream then LEFT. Ignore a path going left just before a wooden gate (the path through the gate leads to a picnic spot). From the gate continue past a model sailing boat (on the right). The boat is named 'Mynach'. Go RIGHT at the next junction and between slate slabs. Bear LEFT alongside Barmouth football ground.

4 Pass a building (on the right) and turn RIGHT through a gateway. Go RIGHT and over a gated level-crossing (*take care here, especially with children*). Cross the road and continue AHEAD along the road opposite. Turn LEFT at the promenade. *The white building on the corner is the Barmouth Coastguard Rescue Station.* Pass the Min y Mor Hotel and the primary school playing field. *The wind turbine here provides electricity for the school.* Cross a road then pass the Arbour Hotel. Turn LEFT into North Avenue then RIGHT into Marine Road. Retrace your steps to the starting point.

GELLFAWR FARM & THE SLABS

DESCRIPTION This 3-mile walk takes you high above Barmouth to some farm ruins in a spectacular situation. You then pass below some dramatic cliffs used for rock climbing. Allow 3 hours.

START Barmouth Railway Station (SH612158). Walk over the level-crossing and turn LEFT.

DIRECTIONS *From the east (A496):* After entering the town, pass the Birmingham Garage and Last Inn public house (both on the right). Immediately after the pub turn LEFT under a railway bridge. Follow the road past the harbour and then, after a right turn, park in Barmouth's main car-park (on the RIGHT).
From the north (A496): Drive through the town, continuing AHEAD at the end of the one-way system to pass St David's Church (on the right). Immediately after the church turn RIGHT under a railway bridge. Follow the road past the harbour and then, after a right turn, park in Barmouth's main car-park (on the RIGHT).
Bus services: Buses X94 (from Bala and Dolgellau) and 38 (from Harlech) serve Barmouth.
Train services: There are trains from Machynlleth, Porthmadog and Pwllheli.

I Walk away from the station, passing Talbot Place on your left. At the first road junction cross the High Street, using the pedestrian crossing, and continue AHEAD into Gellfechan Road. Walk uphill to arrive at St John's Church. *St John's is the biggest church in Barmouth and was built during the 1890s.* Continue uphill on Gellfechan Road to where it meets a way-marked track (on the right). *You are now at the highest point on Gellfechan Road from where there is a wonderful view over Barmouth.* Turn RIGHT and follow the track uphill. *Look to the left as you walk to see the first of three tunnel entrances. This area was once exten-*

sively mined for manganese.

2 Go through the side gate adjoining a metal gate and turn LEFT. Soon you'll pass the second tunnel entrance (on the right) before bearing RIGHT to climb more steeply. When the track divides go LEFT. Pass the third mine entrance (on the right) before going through a metal gate and arriving at the ruins of Gellfechan Farm. *An interesting book about the farm by Carol Skelton, 'Gellfechan and its Last Family', is available-locally.* Pass a barn (on the left) to reach a marker (indicating the Ardudwy Way) at a junction of paths.

3 Go AHEAD here, uphill past another marker and through a wall (ignore a path going left here). Then pass a third marker and go AHEAD, following a path alongside a wall (on the left). Soon the path goes RIGHT and alongside a stream (on the left) to a gap in a wall. Continue AHEAD at the waymark beyond the wall then, soon, bear LEFT to an Ardudwy Way marker and metal gate. Cross a slab bridge before going through the gate. Follow the path LEFT by a rocky outcrop, then RIGHT, to continue alongside a fence (on the right). Bear RIGHT at the next marker and pass a barn (on the left) to arrive at Gellfawr Farm. *This remote farm once had great significance as the settlement closest to the manganese mines which were worked in the hills above it.*

4 Turn RIGHT by the waymark on the barn adjoining Gellfawr and follow the track past the house. Cross a stream and pass another marker (on the right) before reaching a metal gate and stile. Go through/over and continue along a rough tarmac road. Ignore a waymark pointing right and follow the road downhill. *There are wonderful views from here of the Mawddach Estuary and the ridge of Cadair Idris.* Soon, take the marked footpath going RIGHT at a left-hand bend. *The dramatic cliffs above you to the right here are called the Slabs and are often used by rock climbers.* The path goes downhill and through a metal gate in a high wall.

5 Continue downhill, passing mine workings on the left. Go through another metal gate and follow the path LEFT near a wall on the right. Then go RIGHT through a third metal gate. Walk AHEAD at a junction of paths with markers alongside a wooden seat. Soon, go LEFT through a gate marked 'Frenchman's Grave'. Walk downhill then through another gate to the grave. *The Frenchman, Auguste Guyard, settled in Barmouth Old Town. A poem on a plaque marks the site.* Return to the upper gate, go through and turn LEFT onto the path beyond.

6 Soon, go through another gate and AHEAD alongside a wall (on the left) to a road and information board. *You are now at Dinas Oleu (The Fortress of Light), the first site to be donated to the National Trust (in 1895).* Turn RIGHT and follow the road downhill, bearing RIGHT at a junction. After the road turns LEFT go AHEAD over

a cross-roads to arrive at Barmouth High Street. Turn RIGHT here and walk along the High Street. Then, near a Spar shop (on the left), walk over the road, using the pedestrian crossing. Go RIGHT and then LEFT to return to the start.

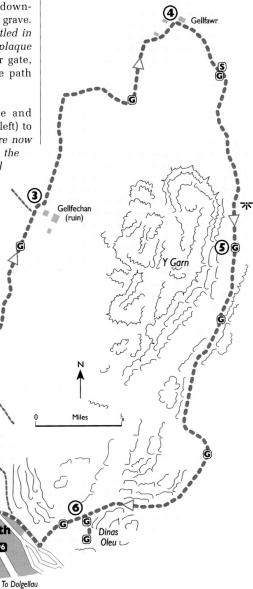

19

THE BIRMINGHAM MONUMENT

DESCRIPTION A 2½-mile walk which takes you on a magical path which winds its way up through dense woodland above Barmouth to one of the town's finest viewpoints. Allow 2½ hours.

START Barmouth Railway Station (SH612158). Walk over the level-crossing and turn LEFT.

DIRECTIONS From the east (A496): After entering the town, pass Barmouth Bridge (on the left) and then the Last Inn public house (on the right). Immediately after the pub turn LEFT under a railway bridge. Follow the road past the harbour and then, after a right turn, park in Barmouth's main car-park (on the RIGHT).

From the north (A496): Drive through the town, continuing AHEAD at the end of the one-way system to pass St David's Church (on the right). Immediately after the church turn RIGHT under a railway bridge. Follow the road past the harbour and then, after a right turn, park in Barmouth's main car-park (on the RIGHT).

Bus services: Buses X94 (from Bala and Dolgellau) and 38 (from Harlech) serve Barmouth.

Train services: There are trains from Machynlleth, Porthmadog and Pwllheli.

I Walk away from the station, passing Talbot Place on your left. At the High Street turn LEFT and follow the left-hand pavement to the first road junction. Turn LEFT here and follow the road past the Co-op Supermarket and Bradbury's Garage. Pass a bridge over the railway (on the left). Take the next road on the RIGHT and walk through a metal gate into the park beyond. Pass the Barmouth War Memorial (on the right) and tennis courts (on the left), then leave the park through another metal gate. Turn LEFT and follow the road alongside the park. Go RIGHT before the entrance to Bryn Mynach (Hill of the Monks) house and walk uphill to a main road (you'll see the Bryn Teg pub to the right across the road).

2 Turn LEFT and follow the road, crossing it when you see a post-box. Turn LEFT and then bear RIGHT onto Ffordd Mynach (Road of the Monks). *This is one of many places in the Barmouth area named after the Cistercian monks of Cymer Abbey, near Dolgellau.* Follow the road uphill, passing two tracks going off to the right and Barmouth Rectory. Turn RIGHT at the first road junction and walk AHEAD to an electricity sub-station. Turn LEFT here through a gateway onto a footpath going uphill. Ignore a faint path up to a house (on the right). Soon, follow a path going RIGHT to a gap in the foliage where there's a good viewpoint. *You can see down the coast to the south from here.*

3 Return to the main path and turn RIGHT, following it up steps and round a series of zigzags as it gains height. Go through a wall and up more steps to arrive at a clearing where the path divides, the left-hand branch going to a metal gate. Turn RIGHT here and follow the path through the trees and up some rock outcrops to the Birmingham Monument. *At this spectacular viewpoint there's a cairn constructed in honour of Birmingham soldiers killed on 1 July 1916, during World War I. A plaque can be found just below the summit on the west of the cairn. The view of Barmouth from here is spectacular and, in good conditions, you can see Bardsey island near the Llŷn Peninsula.*

4 Return, the way you came, to the junction of paths and bear RIGHT to go through the metal gate. Follow the path as it bears HALF-RIGHT through a low wall near some ruined buildings (on the left). Continue AHEAD over relatively level ground past a solitary tree. Then go through another wall to arrive at the end of a barn (on the right) next to a waymark. *The marker indicates that the Ardudwy Way passes here. You are now at the ruins of Gellfechan Farm. Carol Skelton's book about the farm, 'Gellfechan and its Last Family', is available locally.* Turn RIGHT at the waymark and follow the track past the barn and a wooden gate (on the left).

5 Continue down-hill and go through a metal gate. *Soon, look to the left for the first of three tunnel entrances. This area was once extensively mined for manganese.* Ignore a minor path going left then, at a junction of tracks, turn RIGHT by a waymark. Continue down-hill, following the track LEFT (watch for the second tunnel entrance on the left just after the bend). Turn RIGHT at the next junction and walk through the side gate adjoining a metal gate. Go downhill, passing a section of wall (on the right). *Look for the third tunnel entrance just beyond the wall.* After a telegraph pole (on the left) go LEFT down a grassy path to a road. Turn LEFT again and walk downhill to St John's Church. *St John's is the biggest church in Barmouth and was built during the 1890s.* Go RIGHT here and follow the road down to Barmouth High Street. Go over the pedestrian crossing, then RIGHT and LEFT, to return to the start.

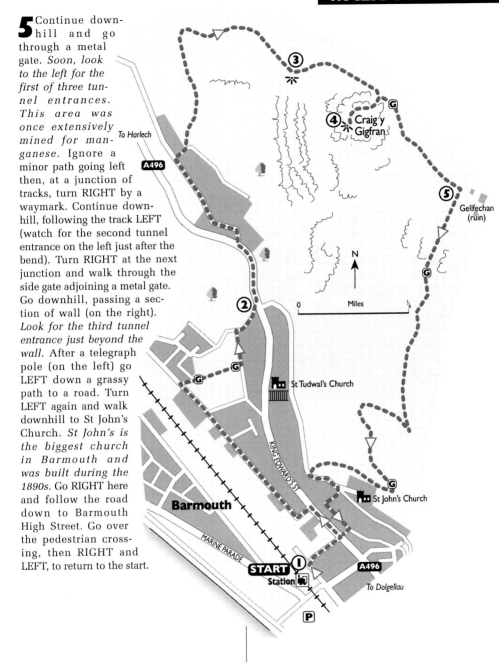

DINAS OLEU & GELLFECHAN FARM

DESCRIPTION An exciting 2½-mile walk which takes you high above Barmouth to a spectacular viewpoint. You then climb even higher, passing the ruins of an old farm and gaining views far out to Bardsey Island and the Llŷn Peninsula. Allow 2½ hours.

START Barmouth Railway Station (SH612158). Walk over the level-crossing and turn LEFT.

DIRECTIONS *From the east (A496):* After entering the town, pass Barmouth Bridge (on the left) and then the Last Inn public house (on the right). Immediately after the pub turn LEFT under a railway bridge. Follow the road past the harbour and then, after a right turn, park in Barmouth's main car-park (on the RIGHT).

From the north (A496): Drive through the town, continuing AHEAD at the end of the one-way system to pass St David's Church (on the right). Immediately after the church turn RIGHT under a railway bridge. Follow the road past the harbour and then, after a right turn, park in Barmouth's main car-park (on the RIGHT).

Bus services: Buses X94 (from Bala and Dolgellau) and 38 (from Harlech) serve Barmouth.

Train services: There are trains from Machynlleth, Porthmadog and Pwllheli.

I Walk away from the station passing Talbot Place on your left. At the first junction turn RIGHT then cross the High Street at the pedestrian crossing and turn RIGHT. Take the first LEFT (Water Street) and follow the road to a crossroads. Go LEFT and uphill, keeping LEFT at a junction and then taking the second marked footpath on the LEFT. Follow a grassy path uphill then turn sharp RIGHT next to a high fence. Continue on a path which zig-zags up steps and steep slopes. Keep LEFT at a junction of paths then, when the, now grassy, path levels off go LEFT up steps to a stone shelter. *This is a National Trust viewpoint, high on the hillside of Dinas*

Oleu, which was the first site to be donated to the Trust (in 1895). A plaque on the wall of the viewpoint commemorates the 100th anniversary of the donation, by philanthropist Fannie Talbot. There are extensive views from here over Barmouth, the Mawddach Estuary, and over Cardigan Bay to Bardsey Island. Below you can see your starting point, Barmouth Station, and the long sandy beach for which Barmouth is famous.

2 Walk uphill from the viewpoint, go through a wooden gate and AHEAD to a track. Turn LEFT and follow the track. Go through a wooden gate, then downhill to a junction and marker. Go RIGHT here and uphill. *This track is way-marked for the Ardudwy Way, a long-distance footpath from Barmouth to Talybont and Harlech.* Pass a mine entrance (on the right). *This area was once extensively mined for manganese.* Then go through a metal gate to arrive at the ruins of Gellfechan Farm. *An interesting book about the farm by Carol Skelton, 'Gellfechan and its Last Family', is available locally.* Pass a barn (on the left) to reach a marker (indicating the Ardudwy Way) at a junction of paths.

3 Go AHEAD here uphill past another marker and through a wall (ignore a path going left here). Then, at a third marker, go RIGHT and follow a path uphill towards a marker above you. Pass this, walk alongside a wall (on the right) and go over a stone stile to a marker. Turn LEFT and walk uphill past a wooden gate in the wall (on the left). *Pause at the top of the rise for a glorious view southwards along the Cardigan Bay coast. The village of Llwyngwril can be seen below the end of the ridge of Cadair Idris and, on a clear day, you can make out the Preseli Mountains, in Pembrokeshire, in the far distance.* Walk downhill alongside the wall on your left, and through a gateway, to a marker. *The farm you can see across the fields is Gellfawr, a remote settlement once at the centre of the manganese mining in the area.* Go LEFT through a wooden gate and follow a track above a stream (on the right) to a gateway in a wall. *From here there is a spectacular view across the sea to the end of the Llŷn Peninsula and Bardsey Island.* Bear LEFT and walk with the wall on your right. *The cairn below to the right is the Birmingham Monument (see Walk 11).*

4 Continue AHEAD at a marker (it was from here that you walked uphill to the stone stile). Then retrace your steps past Gellfechan Farm downhill, through a metal gate, to the junction you walked up from earlier. Turn RIGHT here and continue downhill on a track which bears LEFT past another mine entrance. Bear LEFT at a junction alongside a metal gate (on the right) and go downhill, through a wooden gate. Pass a fence and the beginning of the path you followed up to the National Trust viewpoint (both on the left), and continue down to a road. Turn RIGHT here and retrace your steps to the starting point.

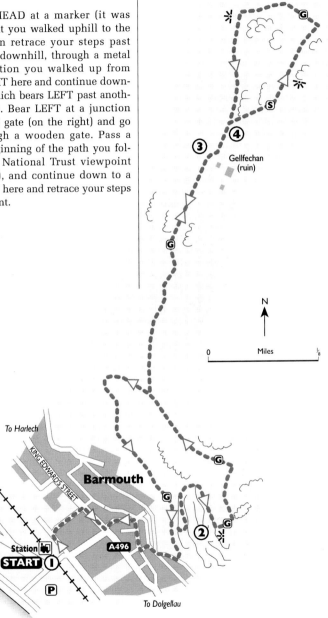

THE OLD TOWN & GORLLWYN FAWR

DESCRIPTION This glorious 2½-mile walk takes you uphill through Barmouth's fascinating Old Town and provides some of the best views in the area. Allow 2 hours.

START Barmouth Railway Station (SH612158). Walk over the level-crossing and turn LEFT.

DIRECTIONS *From the east (A496):* After entering the town, pass Barmouth Bridge (on the left) then the Last Inn public house (on the right). Immediately after the pub turn LEFT under a railway bridge. Follow the road past the harbour and then, after a right turn, park in Barmouth's main car-park (on the RIGHT).
From the north (A496): Drive through the town, continuing AHEAD at the end of the one-way system to pass St David's Church (on the right). Immediately after the church turn RIGHT under a railway bridge. Follow the road past the harbour and then, after a right turn, park in Barmouth's main car-park (on the RIGHT).
Bus services: Buses X94 (from Bala and Dolgellau) and 38 (from Harlech) serve Barmouth.
Train services: There are trains from Machynlleth, Porthmadog and Pwllheli.

1 Walk away from the station, passing Talbot Place on your left. Cross the High Street at the pedestrian crossing and turn RIGHT. Take the first LEFT (Water Street) and follow the road to a cross-roads. Continue AHEAD along Cambrian Street, ignore steps going left, and turn LEFT onto the footpath alongside the High Street. Just after the end of the one-way traffic system take St George's Lane on the LEFT. Go up steps into the Old Town, ignoring more steps going left, and continue to a junction by a lamp-post. Bear LEFT up steps, ignore a path going right in front of Goronwy Cottage, and continue up more steps. Continue past the Williams Buildings (on the left), ignore a path going left, and turn RIGHT up two sets of steps past a path going right.

2 At a junction, ignore the road going left and a path going ahead, but bear LEFT up more steps. *There's a good view from here of the Cadair Idris range and Barmouth Bridge to the south.* Ignore a path going right past a terrace of houses and continue AHEAD up narrower steps. Pass Bwth Carron (on the right), go LEFT and up steps then RIGHT to a sign for 'Mountain Walk'. *There is a plaque here commemorating philanthropist Fannie Talbot's donation of the hillside of Dinas Oleu (Fortress of Light) to the National Trust in 1895.* Turn LEFT and walk uphill, past Ty'n Ffynnon house and a path going left, to an information board about Dinas Oleu. Go uphill from here past a National Trust sign. Bear LEFT at a junction of paths above some steps. At the next junction go RIGHT and uphill, ignoring a path on the left. Walk through a metal gate and alongside a wall (on the right).

3 Soon turn RIGHT through a wooden gate marked 'Frenchman's Grave'. Go downhill to a second gate. The grave is just after this. *The Frenchman, Auguste Guyard, once lived in Barmouth Old Town and a plaque marks his grave.* Return to the upper gate and turn RIGHT onto the path beyond. Follow this alongside the wall (on the right) to a seat. *The views from here over Barmouth Bridge and the Mawddach Estuary are astounding.* Bear RIGHT at a junction of way-marked paths just past the seat and walk downhill to a metal gate. Ignore the path going right and walk through the gate and AHEAD alongside a wall (on the right).

4 Turn LEFT onto a road alongside the entrance to Cae Fadog and walk uphill. Ignore a kissing gate (on the right) and follow the now unsurfaced track past Tregarn house (on the right) to a wooden gate with marker. Walk through to a junction alongside Gorllwyn Fawr (on the right). Bear RIGHT here and walk past the house. Ignore a house entrance (on the left) and continue down a tarmac road, ignoring a track going right, to a junction and marker. Go RIGHT and follow this road downhill to Bryn Melyn Guesthouse.

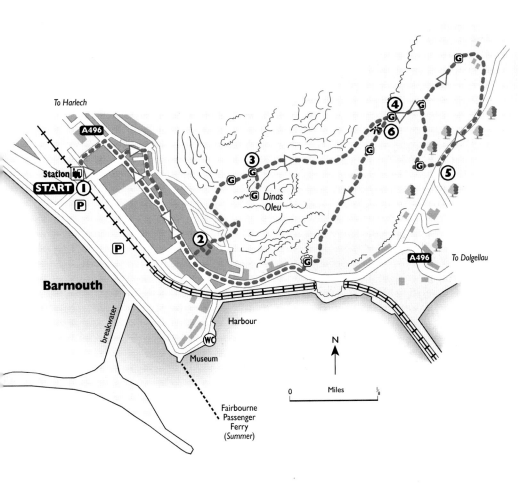

To Harlech

A496

Station

START

P

P

Barmouth

breakwater

Harbour

Museum

WC

Fairbourne
Passenger
Ferry
(Summer)

Dinas
Oleu

N

0   Miles   ⅛

A496

To Dolgellau

5 Pass the entrance to Bryn Melyn and go RIGHT up steps alongside a waymark. Soon the path bends right, passes a gate marked Cae Fadog (on the left) and goes through a metal gate. Pass Cader Betti (on the left) and continue AHEAD onto a road. Bear LEFT at a sign (on the left), walk uphill and cross a parking space. Go LEFT at a marker, uphill and through the kissing gate passed earlier. Turn LEFT and retrace your steps, going RIGHT past the entrance to Cae Fadog and through the metal gate.

6 Now go LEFT downhill, through another metal gate then alongside a wall (on the right). Pass a quarry (on the right), then a marker, before going down through a metal gate. Go RIGHT down steps and between houses to a road and marker. Turn RIGHT and follow the right-hand pavement past the Last Inn to the centre of Barmouth. Turn LEFT over the pedestrian crossing near the Spar shop, then go RIGHT and LEFT to return to the starting point.

CAE FADOG & THE SLABS

DESCRIPTION This 2½-mile walk takes you on a path which climbs from Barmouth harbour to the town's dramatic hinterland. At the highest point of the walk you pass the precipitous cliffs, called the Slabs, used as practice slopes by climbers. Allow 2½ hours.

START Barmouth Railway Station (SH612158). Walk over the level-crossing and turn LEFT.

DIRECTIONS *From the east (A496):* After entering the town, pass Barmouth Bridge (on the left) and then the Last Inn public house (on the right). Immediately after the pub turn LEFT under a railway bridge. Follow the road past the harbour and then, after a right turn, park in Barmouth's main car-park (on the RIGHT).

From the north (A496): Drive through the town, continuing AHEAD at the end of the one-way system to pass St David's Church (on the right). Immediately after the church turn RIGHT under a railway bridge. Follow the road past the harbour and then, after a right turn, park in Barmouth's main car-park (on the RIGHT).

Bus services: Buses X94 (from Bala and Dolgellau) and 38 (from Harlech) serve Barmouth.

Train services: There are trains from Machynlleth, Porthmadog and Pwllheli.

I Walk away from the station, passing Talbot Place on your left. Walk over the High Street at the pedestrian crossing and turn RIGHT. Follow the left-hand pavement past the Tal y Don pub and then through the town. Pass St David's Church (on the right) then The Last Inn (on the left). Go LEFT at a footpath marker and up steps, passing some houses. Walk LEFT through a metal gate and up steps onto a grassy path past a quarry (on the left). Continue uphill alongside a wall (on the left). Then go up steps and through a metal gate near a white house (Cae Fadog Fach) on the right. Go sharp LEFT at a junction of paths and uphill to another junction. *The wooden seat here is well positioned: there are wonderful views*

over the Mawddach Estuary and Barmouth Bridge. Turn sharp RIGHT at the marker here and walk uphill. Go through a metal gate and alongside a stream (on the right).

2 Soon bear HALF-LEFT towards a wall, ignoring a path going right. Then go RIGHT and uphill between rocky outcrops. Go through a metal gate and continue uphill. Pass a mine entrance (up on the right), then walk through another metal gate. Continue alongside cliffs on your left. *There is a good view from here of the upper Mawddach Valley with the Aran Mountains in the distance.* Soon the path reaches a tarmac road, alongside the final section of cliffs, the Slabs. *You may well see climbers practising on these precipitous slopes.* Turn RIGHT and follow the road to a metal gate and stile. Go through/over and downhill, ignoring a way-marked path going left. Pass a track going uphill on the left. Then go RIGHT by a marker just before another house. Walk downhill to a metal gate alongside a barn (on the right).

3 Go through and AHEAD alongside a fence, then a wall (both on the left). Pass waymarks (on the left) and continue AHEAD uphill at a junction of paths. Bear LEFT and walk along the edge of the hillside which falls away to the left. Pass two markers and then follow the path as it dips slightly below the ridge top to arrive at a third marker. Go HALF-RIGHT from here and downhill to a metal gate and marker.

4 Continue above a gully and then alongside a wall. Go through a metal gate and AHEAD. *The hill-top below to the left is the site of the Panorama Walk (see Walk 18).* Pass above a ruined barn and then cross a stream. Turn LEFT at a junction and walk downhill on the path you walked up earlier. Go through a metal gate to the junction by the wooden seat. Go sharp LEFT downhill to a metal gate and marker (ignore the path going right, which you followed earlier). Go through, alongside a wall (on the right) to a road and the entrance to Cae Fadog. Go LEFT uphill to a kissing gate (on the right). Walk through and downhill to a marker and parking space. Cross this and walk downhill alongside a fence and a house to a road.

5 Turn RIGHT, go downhill and to the left of Cader Betti house. Go through a metal gate, ignore an entrance to Cae Fadog and walk downhill alongside Bryn Melyn Guesthouse. Go down steps and turn RIGHT onto a road. Ignore a track going right then bear RIGHT at a black and white marker post. Walk downhill to a road junction then continue AHEAD to a main road. Go RIGHT and follow the right-hand pavement to the steps you walked up earlier. Return from here to the starting point.

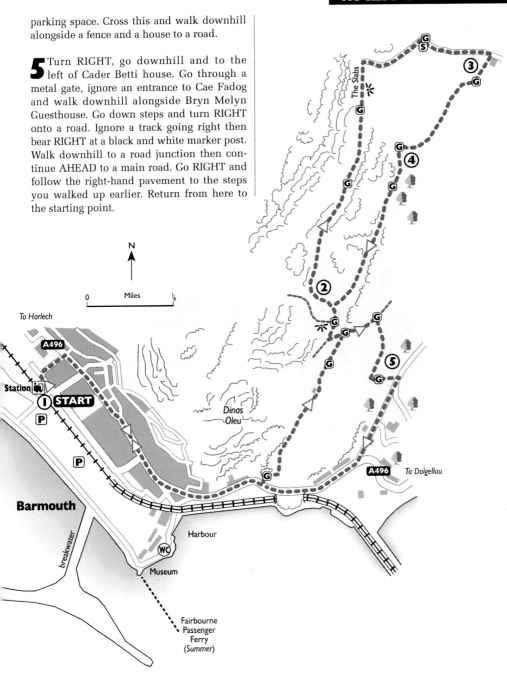

N

0   Miles   ⅛

To Harlech

A496

Station

START

P

P

P

Barmouth

breakwater

Dinas Oleu

The Slabs

③

④

⑤

②

A496 To Dolgellau

Harbour

WC

Museum

Fairbourne
Passenger
Ferry
(Summer)

BARMOUTH BRIDGE & THE MAWDDACH ESTUARY

DESCRIPTION A delightful 3½-mile walk which takes you across Barmouth's railway bridge, with its wonderful views of estuary and mountains. You then follow part of the disused railway line from Dolgellau before returning alongside the Mawddach with views over the estuary back to Barmouth. (Note there's a toll of 90p return [50p for under16s] for access to Barmouth Bridge. Should you wish to catch a train to or from Morfa Mawddach Station [a request stop] do check the times in Barmouth before you start the walk). Allow 3 hours.

START Barmouth Railway Station (SH612158). Walk over the level-crossing and turn LEFT.

DIRECTIONS From the east (A496): After entering the town, pass Barmouth Bridge (on the left) and then the Last Inn public house (on the right). Immediately after the pub turn LEFT under a railway bridge. Follow the road past the harbour and then, after a right turn, park in Barmouth's main car-park (on the RIGHT).

From the north (A496): Drive through the town, continuing AHEAD at the end of the one-way system to pass St David's Church (on the right). Immediately after the church turn RIGHT under a railway bridge. Follow the road past the harbour and then, after a right turn, park in Barmouth's main car-park (on the RIGHT).

Bus services: Buses X94 (from Bala and Dolgellau) and 38 (from Harlech) serve Barmouth.

Train services: There are trains from Machynlleth, Porthmadog and Pwllheli.

1 With your back to the station, turn RIGHT and then RIGHT again to go over the level crossing. Continue AHEAD until you reach the promenade. Cross the road and turn LEFT here. Pass Barmouth Coastguard Station (on the left) and then the Bath House

café (on the right). Follow the road past the harbour and under a railway bridge. Cross the main road just after the bridge and turn RIGHT. Follow the left-hand pavement past the Last Inn (on the left) and alongside the road as it bends right and left. Cross the road (*take care here, especially with children*) to the entrance to Barmouth Bridge on the RIGHT. Walk downhill to the toll-booth.

2 Continue AHEAD, walking alongside the section of the railway bridge designed to swing to allow ships access to the Mawddach. *Barmouth Bridge was opened in 1867 and was fitted with its existing metal swinging span in 1900. The bridge was closed in 1980 when it was discovered that the wooden piles supporting it were infested with a voracious marine wood-worm. The bridge was made safe and re-opened in 1986. Today it carries trains every two hours on weekdays north to Pwllheli and south to Machynlleth. There are wonderful views of the Mawddach estuary and of the surrounding mountains from the bridge.* Go through a metal gate at the bridge end and continue AHEAD.

3 Soon cross a stream, after which ignore marked footpaths going left and right, and an entrance to the platform at Morfa Mawddach station, before joining the Mawddach Trail (the former Dolgellau-

Barmouth railway line). *Known originally as Barmouth Junction, this station was where the railway line from Dolgellau joined the Cambrian Coast line. The station was busy then and provided a café for passengers changing trains. The Dolgellau to Barmouth railway walk featured in Julia Bradbury's 2008 BBC television series. Her book about it is available from*

Go through and downhill to a track. Turn LEFT and follow the track alongside the Mawddach Estuary. *This area was used by the military during the Second World War, hence the remains of concrete bunkers near the track.* Soon the track divides. Go LEFT here, by a marker, and then RIGHT, past another marker, to walk behind a terrace of houses. *This is Mawddach Crescent, built in the 1890s by businessman Solomon Andrews, who hoped to create a holiday resort to rival Barmouth.*

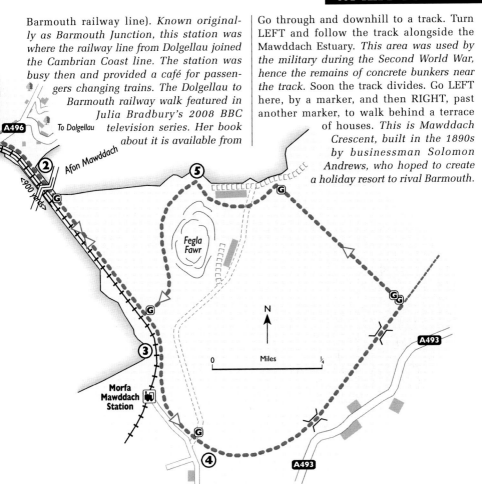

Frances Lincoln Publishers. The trail takes you behind the remains of the old station's Dolgellau platforms then past public toilets (on the left). Ignore a road (on the right) and continue AHEAD on the tarmac path. Walk between wooden posts and cross a road to go AHEAD through a metal gate (marked Cycle Route 8) to follow the trail.

4 Ignore minor paths going left and right, and cross two bridges before arriving at a footpath which crosses the trail. Go LEFT here, and follow the path through a wooden gate, then a metal gate. Pass a metal seat (on the left) and, soon after, walk uphill to a wooden gate, ignoring a path going right.

5 The path rejoins the estuary at the end of the crescent and bears LEFT alongside a rocky outcrop (to the right). *There is a particularly good view of Barmouth Bridge from here.* Follow the track LEFT after a length of wall (on the right) and then over an embankment. At a second embankment turn RIGHT and follow a path along it to a metal gate and markers. Go through and turn RIGHT to return over Barmouth Bridge. *Should you wish to catch a train back to Barmouth go LEFT, then RIGHT to Morfa Mawddach station.* Once over the bridge retrace your steps to the starting point.

GELLFAWR FARM & LLANABER

DESCRIPTION An exciting 5-mile walk which provides you with magnificent views over Cardigan Bay. It then takes you past an ancient hill-fort and a medieval church before you return to Barmouth along the promenade. Allow 4 hours.

START Barmouth Railway Station (SH612158). Walk over the level-crossing and turn LEFT.

DIRECTIONS *From the east (A496):* After entering the town, pass Barmouth Bridge (on the left) and then the Last Inn public house (on the right). Immediately after the pub turn LEFT under a railway bridge. Follow the road past the harbour and then, after a right turn, park in Barmouth's main car-park (on the RIGHT).

From the north (A496): Drive through the town, continuing AHEAD at the end of the one-way system to pass St David's Church (on the right). Immediately after the church turn RIGHT under a railway bridge. Follow the road past the harbour and then, after a right turn, park in Barmouth's main car-park (on the RIGHT).

Bus services: Buses X94 (from Bala and Dolgellau) and 38 (from Harlech) serve Barmouth.

Train services: There are trains from Machynlleth, Porthmadog and Pwllheli.

I Walk away from the station, past Talbot Place to the High Street. Walk over the pedestrian crossing and turn RIGHT. Pass the Tal y Don pub and take the next road LEFT. Go AHEAD at a cross-roads and uphill. Bear LEFT at a junction and take the second marked footpath going LEFT. Ignore a path going right, go through a wooden gate and bear RIGHT at a junction of tracks. Pass a mine entrance (on the right). *This area was once extensively mined for manganese.* When the track divides go LEFT and uphill. Pass a second mine entrance (on the right) then go through a metal gate to Gellfechan Farm. *Carol Skelton's book, 'Gellfechan and its Last Family', is available locally.* Pass a

barn (on the left) and a marker at a junction.

2 Continue past another marker and through a wall (ignore a path going left here). Then, at a third marker, continue AHEAD. Go RIGHT, alongside a stream (on the left) then through a gateway to a way-mark. Continue AHEAD but, soon, bear LEFT to a marker and metal gate. Go over a bridge and through the gate. Follow the path LEFT then RIGHT, continuing alongside a fence (on the right). Bear RIGHT at the next marker to reach Gellfawr Farm. *This remote settlement is close to the manganese mines which were worked in the hills above it.* Turn LEFT at Gellfawr and follow a track past waymarks then through a gateway and alongside a wall (on the left). Ignore a track going left and continue to a junction and markers.

3 Go LEFT here and through a gateway above a ruin. Follow the track RIGHT (ignore a track going left) and uphill to a metal gate and marker. *There are now magnificent views northwards to the Llŷn Peninsula.* Go through and pass a manganese working going left. Soon, go LEFT at markers and downhill through a metal gate. Go LEFT at a marker, walk uphill and bear LEFT alongside a marker. Go through/over a metal gate/stile and downhill (ignore a gate on the right). *To the left here there's a mining incline. On the hilltop ahead are the remains of the Bronze Age Llanaber Fort.* Walk downhill through a wooden gate. Ignore a wooden gate (on the left) and continue alongside a fence (also on the left). Pass a metal gate (on the left). Soon go though/over a metal gate/style and turn LEFT. Follow a marked track through a metal gate and between walls. Ignore gateways to left and right as you continue.

4 Go AHEAD across a field then through/over a metal gate/stile and downhill alongside a fence (on the right). Pass a private track going left and continue past gateways down a marked track. Cross a stile by a closed gate and markers. Then pass a marker (on the right) and immediately turn LEFT at a junction. Go downhill past another marker. Ignoring field entrances, go through a metal

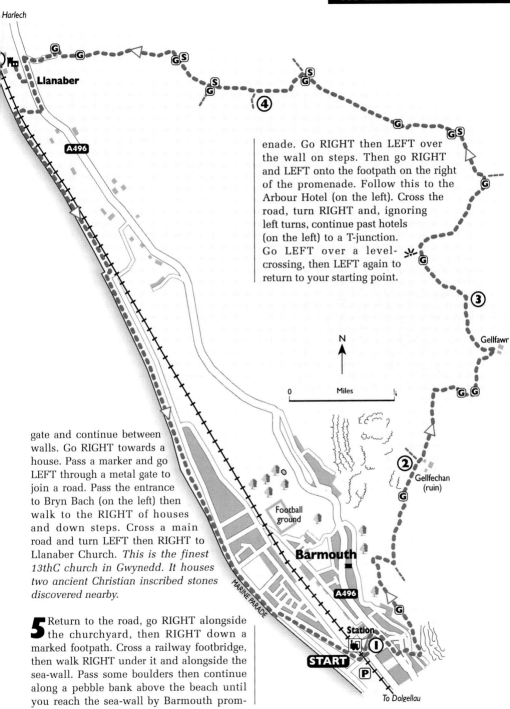

enade. Go RIGHT then LEFT over the wall on steps. Then go RIGHT and LEFT onto the footpath on the right of the promenade. Follow this to the Arbour Hotel (on the left). Cross the road, turn RIGHT and, ignoring left turns, continue past hotels (on the left) to a T-junction. Go LEFT over a level-crossing, then LEFT again to return to your starting point.

gate and continue between walls. Go RIGHT towards a house. Pass a marker and go LEFT through a metal gate to join a road. Pass the entrance to Bryn Bach (on the left) then walk to the RIGHT of houses and down steps. Cross a main road and turn LEFT then RIGHT to Llanaber Church. *This is the finest 13thC church in Gwynedd. It houses two ancient Christian inscribed stones discovered nearby.*

5 Return to the road, go RIGHT alongside the churchyard, then RIGHT down a marked footpath. Cross a railway footbridge, then walk RIGHT under it and alongside the sea-wall. Pass some boulders then continue along a pebble bank above the beach until you reach the sea-wall by Barmouth prom-

ORIELTON WOODS

DESCRIPTION A fascinating 3-mile walk which takes you on a delightful footpath through Orielton Woods, visiting some spectacular viewpoints overlooking the Mawddach Estuary en route. Allow 2½ hours

START The car-park on the A496 at Orielton Woods (SH623157).

DIRECTIONS *From the east (A496):* Just before entering Barmouth pass (on the left) a large house with a clocktower and, soon after, drive into the Orielton Woods car-park (on the RIGHT).

From the north (A496): Drive through the town, continuing AHEAD at the end of the one-way system to pass St David's Church (on the right) and the Last Inn (on the left). After several bends follow the road downhill and drive into the Orielton Woods car-park (on the LEFT).

Bus services: Buses X94 (from Bala and Dolgellau) and 38 (from Harlech) serve Barmouth.

Train services: There are trains from Machynlleth, Porthmadog and Pwllheli.

Orielton Woods car-park is on the X94 bus route and about a 15-minute walk from Barmouth station along the Dolgellau road (A496).

1 Enter Orielton Woods through a wooden gate. *This forested ravine was originally landscaped during the early 19thC. It is home to a large variety of plant and bird species. The stainless steel sculpture over to the right is a representation of a pre-historic trilobite which once lived in Gwynedd.* Bear RIGHT to cross a bridge over the stream, then go RIGHT again to reach the sculpture and information board. Return to the main path and turn RIGHT up some steps. Soon, follow the path LEFT, across a second bridge and then RIGHT. Continue up the path to where it divides. Turn RIGHT and go over the third bridge to follow the path uphill. Bear RIGHT at the next junction, where steps go uphill left, and pass a notice indicating a steep drop

to the right. The path is narrower now and takes you a short distance to a viewpoint. *There are magnificent views from here over Barmouth Bridge to the village of Fairbourne and out to sea.*

2 Return past the notice, ignoring the steps going right, downhill to the third bridge. Cross the bridge and turn RIGHT. *There's a convenient shelter and picnic table here.* Follow the path as it then turns sharply LEFT uphill, then RIGHT (ignore a faint path going left at this point). The path passes through a gap between walls. It then continues uphill alongside a wall (on the right) to meet a tarmac road where there's a signpost to the Panorama Walk (see Walk 18). Turn LEFT onto the road and follow it past a driveway (on the right) to a footpath sign pointing right. Go sharp RIGHT here, passing signs to several houses including Cae Fadog. Ignore the entrance to Llwyn Celyn (on the right) and continue AHEAD on a stony track which passes between the end of Gorllwyn Fawr and a barn to its right.

3 Follow the walled track to the LEFT (ignore a grass track going right at this point) and go through a wooden gate with a marker. Pass the entrance to Tregarn house (on the left) and a kissing gate (on the left). Then continue downhill to the gateway to Cae Fadog. Turn RIGHT here and follow a grass track alongside a wall to a metal gate. Go through the gate and turn LEFT, ignoring a path going right. Soon, go through another metal gate and down steps, before the path bears RIGHT alongside Cae Fadog Fach. Follow the path downhill past the remains of a barn (on the right). Soon you arrive at the remains of a quarry where there are almost perpendicular cliffs to the right. *There are spectacular views from here over Barmouth Harbour and out to sea.* Pass a yellow marker, bear left and descend to a metal gate. Go RIGHT here and down a long flight of steps between houses to arrive at a main road and waymark.

4 Turn LEFT onto the footpath here. Cross the road when you see an opening in the wall and green footpath sign on the right.

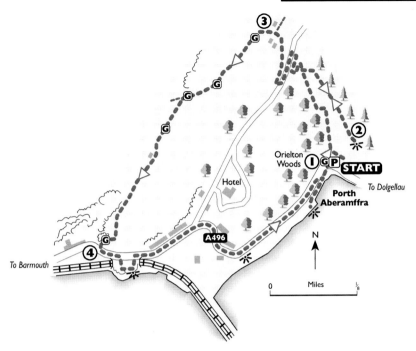

Go through to a viewpoint. *There are good views from here of Barmouth Bridge and over the harbour.* Go LEFT, then LEFT again to return to the main road. Turn RIGHT (*take care, as this is a busy road*) and join the right-hand pavement, alongside the entrance to Barmouth Bridge (see Walk 15). Continue AHEAD passing Porkington Terrace (on the left). *These grand houses date from the heyday of Barmouth tourism, when thousands arrived by train for their holidays.* Ignore a minor road going left as you continue uphill. Pass Penrallt House (on the right) and follow the main road LEFT downhill. *Soon there's another viewpoint (on the right). From here you can see the summit of Cadair Idris towering over the Mawddach Estuary.*

5 Ignore a footpath sign (on the right) and pass Aberamffra Cottage. Then follow the road down to a right-hand bend. Turn RIGHT through a pedestrian gate here to visit Porth Aberamffra. *This was once a busy harbour and ship-building yard. Indeed, during 1867 over 150 ships used the port.* Retrace your steps through the gate. Carefully cross the road to return to your starting point.

Barmouth Bridge

WALK 18

PANORAMA WALK

DESCRIPTION On this 2½-mile walk you visit one of Barmouth's most famous viewpoints from where there are spectacular views of Cadair Idris and much of the Mawddach Estuary. Allow 3 hours.

START The car-park on the A496 at Orielton Woods (SH623157).

DIRECTIONS *From the east (A496):* Just before entering Barmouth pass (on the left) a large house with a clocktower and, soon after, drive into the Orielton Woods car-park (on the RIGHT).

From the north (A496): Drive through the town, continuing AHEAD at the end of the one-way system to pass St David's Church (on the right) and the Last Inn (on the left). After several bends follow the road downhill and drive into the Orielton Woods car-park (on the LEFT).

Bus services: Buses X94 (from Bala and Dolgellau) and 38 (from Harlech) serve Barmouth.

Train services: There are trains from Machynlleth, Porthmadog and Pwllheli.

Orielton Woods car-park is on the X94 bus route and about a 15-minute walk from Barmouth station along the Dolgellau road (A496).

1 Cross the road alongside the car-park *(take care here, especially with children)*. Then walk through the pedestrian gate opposite to visit Porth Aberamffra. *This was once a busy harbour and ship-building yard. Indeed, during 1867 over 150 ships used the port.* Retrace your steps through the gate and turn LEFT onto the left-hand footpath alongside the road. Pass Aberamffra Cottage and ignore a footpath sign (on the left). *Soon there's a viewpoint (on the left). From here you can see the summit of Cadair Idris towering over the Mawddach Estuary.*

2 Continue on the pavement past Penrallt House (on the left). Walk downhill and carefully cross the road to join Panorama Road, on the RIGHT. *The row of large terraced houses on the left here is called Porkington Terrace. These grand houses date from the heyday of Barmouth tourism, when thousands arrived by train for their holidays.* Walk uphill, going AHEAD when Panorama Road bears right. Pass Eithinog house and continue on a path which re-joins Panorama Road. Go LEFT, ignore a track going left then go LEFT onto a marked footpath. Walk up steps alongside Bryn Melyn Guesthouse. Soon the path bends right, passes a gate marked Cae Fadog (on the left) and then goes through a metal gate. Pass Cader Betti (on the left) and continue AHEAD onto a road. Bear LEFT at a sign (on the left), walk uphill and cross a parking space. Go LEFT at a marker, uphill and through a kissing gate.

3 Turn RIGHT onto the track beyond. Follow the track past Tregarn (on the right) and through a wooden gate with marker to a junction by Gorllwyn Fawr. Turn LEFT along a grassy track through a wooden gate. Ignore a track going right and walk uphill between walls. Pass Gorllwyn Fach (on the right) and bear RIGHT at a junction of paths. Go through a metal gate by a waymark and down steps to a track. Turn LEFT and walk downhill to a road. Turn LEFT and walk uphill on the road, ignoring tracks to left and right. Pass Hafod y Bryn (on the right) then go RIGHT, through a metal gate, onto a path signposted 'Panorama'. Walk past a barn (on the right) then uphill and between walls to a wooden gate. Go through, then RIGHT through a metal gate alongside another signpost.

4 Follow the path uphill until it divides. Go LEFT here and up steps. Continue on the path, passing a seat, to arrive at Barmouth's most famous viewpoint. *From here you can see the ridge of Cadair Idris, much of the Mawddach Estuary and Barmouth Bridge. To the east, in the distance, are the Aran Mountains. And the villages of Fairbourne and Llwyngwril can be made out southwards along the coast.* Continue AHEAD along the summit ridge then go RIGHT and down steps to descend behind the summit. Bear LEFT at a junction

To Barm

onto the path you followed uphill earlier. Then retrace your steps to the road (remember to turn LEFT after the first gate). Go LEFT onto the road and downhill, passing Hafod y Bryn and the track from Gorllwyn Fach. Continue along the road, then go LEFT onto a downhill path signposted for Barmouth.

5 Ignore a path going right when the main footpath bends LEFT then RIGHT, passing a picnic table. *You are now in Orielton Woods, in a ravine which falls steeply to the Mawddach Estuary.* Ignore a path going left over a bridge and continue AHEAD down steps alongside a stream. Pass a seat (on the right) and another bridge (on the left). Ignore steps on the right but continue AHEAD on the main path down steps. Go LEFT over a bridge then RIGHT down steps to a junction. *Go LEFT here to visit a stainless steel sculpture of a pre-historic Gwynedd trilobite.* Return to the junction and turn LEFT. Walk over another bridge then go LEFT down steps and through a wooden gate to your starting point.

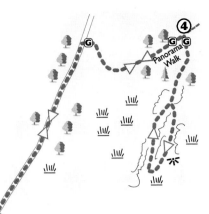

Near Gorllwyn Fawr

LLANABER & FFRIDD FECHAN

DESCRIPTION This 2-mile walk follows a stone and shingle causeway (or, if the tide is out, the beach) to Llanaber, with its ancient church. You then walk up into the hills above the church to pass the old settlement of Ffridd Fechan from where there are magnificent views over Barmouth Bay. Allow 2 hours.

START The car-park at the north end of Barmouth promenade (SH603173).

DIRECTIONS *From the east (A496):* After entering the town, pass Barmouth Bridge (on the left) and then the Last Inn public house (on the right). Immediately after the pub turn LEFT under a railway bridge. Follow the road past the harbour and then, after a right turn, continue along the promenade to its end. Turn round at the mini-roundabout and drive into the car-park AHEAD.

From the north (A496): Drive through the town, continuing AHEAD at the end of the one-way system to pass St David's Church (on the right). Immediately after the church turn RIGHT under a railway bridge. Follow the road past the harbour and then, after a right turn, continue along the promenade to its end. Turn round at the mini-roundabout and drive into the car-park AHEAD.

Bus services: Buses X94 (from Bala and Dolgellau) and 38 (from Harlech) serve Barmouth.

Train services: There are trains from Machynlleth, Porthmadog and Pwllheli.

The north promenade car-park is about a 15-minute walk from Barmouth station along the promenade.

I Walk back past the mini-roundabout and cross the sea-wall ahead of you using the steps provided. Bear RIGHT then LEFT, and walk AHEAD along the top of the shingle bank beside the railway line (to the right). Soon join a concrete path alongside the sea-wall (on the left) and follow the path to a footbridge over the railway. Go over this bridge and follow the path beyond it up to a main road. Turn LEFT and follow the road past Llanaber Church. *St Bodfan's & St Mary's Church is the finest 13thC church in Gwynedd. It houses two ancient Christian inscribed stones discovered in the locality.* Carefully cross the road just after the church. Go up some steps and through a gateway onto a tarmac road.

2 Follow the road uphill, passing a metal gate (on the left). Pass the entrance to Bryn Bach (on the right) and go through a metal gate where the tarmac stops. Turn sharp RIGHT after the gate and follow a track going uphill past a footpath sign. Ignore gates to left and right after the track bears left. Go through a metal gate and follow the track uphill between walls, again ignoring gates and/or gateways into adjoining fields. Go RIGHT at a junction of tracks, passing a yellow arrow which is painted on a wall. Follow the track up to a closed metal gate and stile, then continue uphill beyond it, ignoring a private track going right. Continue to another gate, this one with a stile to the right.

3 Go through/over and follow the track uphill. *Notice the massive clearance cairn over to the right.* Soon pass a heap of boulders (on the left) before turning sharp RIGHT, alongside a wooden gatepost, onto a track going downhill between walls. Ignore a fastened gate on the left and continue down to a junction of tracks. *The house over the wall to the left is Ffridd Fechan and the ruin beyond it is Hafotty. The latter gave its name to the productive manganese mine which was worked on the hill above the farm.* Continue AHEAD here, passing a gateway in the wall on your left, to descend, again between walls.

4 Soon the path goes down more steeply to arrive at a junction. *Pause on the way down to admire the extensive views over northern Barmouth and Cardigan Bay.* Ignore a path going left and continue downhill, passing a metal gate and style where there is a waymark. Continue HALF-RIGHT downhill, crossing a stream twice. Soon after

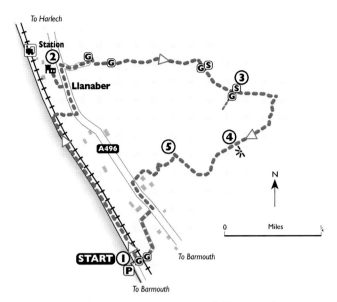

you'll see another metal gate below you on the left. Before reaching it turn RIGHT and follow a path alongside a wall on your left.

5 Soon turn sharp LEFT and follow the narrow path between walls downhill past a house (immediately to the left) to a track. Turn RIGHT alongside a metal gate and follow the track downhill between walls. Pass buildings to left and right, then continue to follow what has now become a road downhill. *After a right turn you'll see the house Tai Croesion on the right.* Soon after, the road meets the main Barmouth to Harlech road.

6 Carefully cross the main road and turn LEFT along the right-hand pavement. Then, opposite a sign for Dryll y Car, turn RIGHT onto a road which is waymarked for the Wales Coast Path. Follow the road downhill between walls. Pass Talafor house (on the right) and continue downhill, going LEFT alongside a metal gate (on the right). *There's a good view from here of the end of the Cadair Idris ridge to the south.* Ignore steps going left through a wall (on the left) and follow the road RIGHT past a house (on the right) to a level-crossing. Go through the pedestrian gates (*take care here, especially with children*). Then turn LEFT to return past the mini-roundabout to your car.

Fridd Fechan

37

WALK 20

ABOVE LLANABER

DESCRIPTION This varied 2-mile walk takes you up into the hills above Llanaber, just to the north of Barmouth. It provides wonderful views over the coastal region and out to the Llŷn Peninsula. Allow 2 hours.

START The car-park at the north end of Barmouth promenade (SH603173).

DIRECTIONS *From the east (A496):* After entering the town, pass Barmouth Bridge (on the left) and then the Last Inn public house (on the right). Immediately after the pub turn LEFT under a railway bridge. Follow the road past the harbour and then, after a right turn, continue along the promenade to its end. Turn round at the mini-roundabout and drive into the car-park AHEAD.

From the north (A496): Drive through the town, continuing AHEAD at the end of the one-way system to pass St David's Church (on the right). Immediately after the church turn RIGHT under a railway bridge. Follow the road past the harbour and then, after a right turn, continue along the promenade to its end. Turn round at the mini-roundabout and drive into the car-park AHEAD.

Bus services: Buses X94 (from Bala and Dolgellau) and 38 (from Harlech) serve Barmouth.

Train services: There are trains from Machynlleth, Porthmadog and Pwllheli.

The north promenade car-park is about a 15-minute walk from Barmouth station along the promenade.

I With your back to the mini-roundabout walk to the Barmouth end of the car-park. Turn LEFT onto a footpath and follow it over a level-crossing through metal pedestrian gates (*take care here, especially with children*). Walk between fences then AHEAD, ignoring a footpath and road going right, and a campsite entrance (on the left). Continue AHEAD through a metal gate and pass Felin Ceilwart house (on the right).

Ceilwart is one of several houses with this name in the immediate locality. You'll pass Ceilwart Cottage later on the walk. Go uphill as the path widens to become a road. Then go LEFT onto a footpath which takes you to a main road. Carefully cross this road and take the minor road opposite, where there's a wooden gate, a waymark and a sign for Ceilwart-Isaf. Follow the road uphill, ignoring the entrance to Ceilwart Cottage (on the left).

2 Soon go LEFT through a metal gate by a waymark. Bear RIGHT and walk uphill by a stream alongside a wall. Pass two gates in the wall and bear LEFT down a tarmac ramp. Then go HALF-RIGHT across a road, passing the entrance to Ceilwart Cottage, and up steps to a metal gate and marker. Go through and RIGHT, crossing the stream on a slab bridge before bearing LEFT to follow the wall (on the right) uphill to a stile and marker. Cross the stile and turn LEFT to follow the wall uphill. Soon there's a yellow marker on a tree. Cross the stream then pass the marker (on the left) and follow the path steeply uphill through trees and then bracken. After a muddy patch you'll come to a stile over the wall, and a gateway through it, on the left where there's also a yellow marker.

3 Go LEFT alongside a wall (on the left), passing another marker. Continue AHEAD along a level trackway which veers away from the wall *Pause here to admire the magnificent view over Barmouth and the coast to the south. You can also make out Llanaber Church below, and Bardsey Island and the Llŷn Peninsula to the north-west.* Soon you'll arrive at another stile alongside a metal gate. Go through/over and LEFT downhill the short distance to a smaller metal gate and marker on your LEFT. Go through this gate and walk downhill near to a wall (on the right). The path parallels the wall, veering left, crossing a stream and then veering right. Continue alongside the wall on the right, passing some metal fencing (on the left). Soon go across the stream again, passing a marker (on the left).

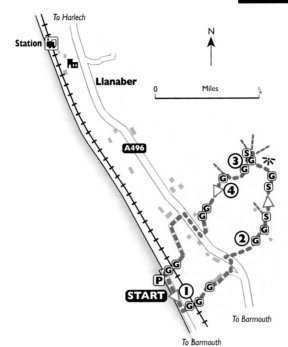

To Harlech

Station

Llanaber

A496

N

0   Miles   ¼

③
④
②
①
START
P

To Barmouth

To Barmouth

4 Continue downhill alongside the wall (on the right) and then make for a metal gate on the LEFT with a marker. Go through and follow the path, now narrowly confined between walls, downhill towards a terrace of houses. Soon the gap between the walls widens sufficiently to accommodate a track. Pass a gateway (on the right) and then go through two metal gates, ignoring a gateway on the left, to arrive at the lane behind the houses. Turn LEFT here and follow the lane down to a main road. Go RIGHT and follow the footpath alongside the road for a short distance to the point where a minor road goes off to the left opposite a sign for Dryll y Car.

5 Carefully cross the main road to join this road, which is waymarked for the Wales Coast Path. Follow the road downhill between walls. Pass Talafor house (on the right) and continue downhill, going LEFT alongside a gate (on the right). *There's a good view from here of the end of the Cadair Idris ridge to the south.* Ignore steps going left through a wall on the left and follow the road RIGHT past a house (on the right) to a level-crossing. Go through the pedestrian gates (*take care here, especially with children*). Then turn LEFT to return past the mini-roundabout, to the starting point.

The coast at Llanaber

PRONUNCIATION

Welsh	English equivalent
c	always hard, as in cat
ch	as in the Scottish word loch
dd	as th in then
f	as f in of
ff	as ff in off
g	always hard as in got
ll	no real equivalent. It is like 'th' in then, but with an 'L' sound added to it, giving 'thlan' for the pronunciation of the Welsh 'Llan'.

In Welsh the accent usually falls on the last-but-one syllable of a word.

KEY TO THE MAPS

- ➛ Walk route and direction
- ▬ Metalled road
- --- Unsurfaced road
- •••• Footpath/route adjoining walk route
- ⤳ River/stream
- ♣ ♤ Trees
- ▬■ Railway
- **G** Gate
- **S** Stile
- **F.B.** Footbridge
- ⸌⸍ Viewpoint
- P Parking
- T Telephone

THE COUNTRYSIDE CODE

- Be safe – plan ahead and follow any signs
- Leave gates and property as you find them
- Protect plants and animals, and take your litter home
- Keep dogs under close control
- Consider other people

Open Access

Some routes cross areas of land where walkers have the legal right of access under The CRoW Act 2000 introduced in May 2005. Access can be subject to restrictions and closure for land management or safety reasons for up to 28 days a year. Details from: www.naturalresourceswales.gov.uk.
Please respect any notices.

About the author, Michael Burnett

Michael is a musician who has written articles and presented radio programmes about Welsh traditional music. He is also the author of three other Kittiwake guides: The Rhinogs, East of Snowdon and Coed y Brenin.

Michael's links to Wales go back to his teenage years when he regularly stayed with friends near Maentwrog and to the 1970s when he lived with his wife, Paula, and their two young children at Blaen Myherin, a remote farmhouse above Devil's Bridge which has now, sadly, become a ruin. Today Michael and Paula share an old farmhouse near the northern Rhinog ridge.

Published by **Kittiwake-Books Limited**
3 Glantwymyn Village Workshops, Glantwymyn, Machynlleth, Montgomeryshire SY20 8LY

© Text & map research: Michael Burnett 2013/2017
© Maps: Kittiwake-Books Ltd 2013

Cover photos: Main: Barmouth Harbour.
Inset: The Old Jail, Barmouth. *David Perrott*

Printed by Mixam, UK.

ISBN: **978 1 908748 07 2**